World of Color

Amaya Jones

ASTA
PUBLICATIONS

ISBN: 978-1-934947-99-9

Artwork and Illustrations provided by:
How Great Thou Art Designs, LLC
Artists: Adrian and Sylvia Jones

Printed in the United States of America

Dedication

To my family for encouraging me to write, especially my Uncle Jabari Jones, one of my biggest influencers.

To my grandfather, Jonathan Jones, for making this book possible. And to my Aunt Jamila Jones, in whose memory one of these poems was written.

I love you all.

Amaya Jones

Table of Contents

Red

Red
Blood gushing from my wound,
Lipstick that compliments any shade
of woman,
A rose from one's true love,
The cry of rage,
Fire blazing in its place,
Sirens wailing in the night air,
Juicy strawberries.
Pit-filled cherries, Delicious apples,
Satin pajamas,
A ladybug's back,
A mesmerizing sunrise,
Red can spark love and passion.

<u>Orange</u>

Orange
Monarchs migrating south, Nemo,
Marlin, and Coral, Daylilies in bloom,
Orange juice poured into a morning's
glass,
The crunch of autumn leaves,
Sparks crackling around a fire,
Saccharine carrots.
Sugary sweet potato pie,
Tangy mandarins,
Tufts of a Truffula tree,
A summer's day,
The sky after a storm,
Orange fills you with vibrancy and zest.

Yellow

Yellow
The sun shining down on me,
McDonald's grand arches, Smiley
face stickers,
Children laughing,
Babies cooing, Puppies playing,
A freshly poured glass of lemonade.
Soft bananas,
Sweet bell peppers,
Giddiness,
A sunny day,
My dress for mom's wedding,
Yellow brings out your true happiness.

<u>Green</u>

Green
My birthstone the emerald,
Leaves clinging to the mighty trees,
Elphaba in all her grace,
A remark of envy,
Cars burning rubber,
Woodland creatures calling out to
the world, Sour Granny Smith Apples.
Crunchy celery sticks, Leafy broccoli,
The soft grass beneath my toes
Seaweed entangling my ankle, Moist
moss on rocks,
Green shows you nature in the flesh.

Blue

Blue
The sky up above,
Blue Morpho butterflies, La Grotta
Azzurra,
The sobbing of the banshee,
La Llorona calling for her children,
My weeping for Jamila,
Delicious blueberry pie. Sour Blowpops,
Juicy Jolly Ranchers,
The cool waters of the majestic falls,
The tears of angels,
Magic of the night,
Blue brings the beauty out of sadness.

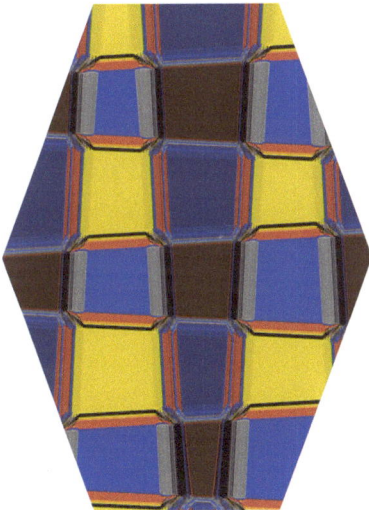

Indigo

Indigo
A twilight sky,
A flower for your jeans,
A skirt twirling with each spin,
 Friends in friendly banter,
The cry of the cosmos, Oms of
meditation, Sweet blackberry jam.
Staining blueberries, Tart plums,
An early morning breeze, Hugs from
a friend,
The squeeze of a Care Bear,
Indigo evokes a sense of peace and serenity.

Violet

The sky of dusk,
A dramatic motion picture, The butterfly
for Jamila, Sisters in playful singing,
My alarm calmly urging me to rise,
Petals flowing in the wind, Thick cough
syrup. Seedless grapes,
Auntie Jean's blackberry cobbler,
Lavender swaying in a field, Serenity,
Orchid petals in my hand,
Violet creates beautiful simplicity.

<u>Pink</u>

Pinkie Pie's curly mane, My mother's
nails,
A good friend named Piglet,
The sound of hope,
Gypsy Bard,
Lots and lots of tickles, Chewy
bubblegum. Frozen strawberry yogurt,
Crunchy frosted animal crackers,
A pretty cocktail dress,
Fluffy feather boas,
An itchy wig fighting for the cure,
Pink is the color of absolute joy.

Brown

The hair upon my head,
Cowboy boots made for a southern gal,
Bark of the mighty trees,
Voices shouting Black Lives Matter,
The battle cry for change,
Chants for a dance, German chocolate cake.
Mom's meatloaf,
Warm chocolate chip cookies,
The earth beneath my feet,
Squishy mud between my fingers,
My smooth skin,
Brown shows the beauty of a continent.

Black

The face of Death himself, Leather
belts on the door, An eternal abyss,
Wails of the dead,
Matter being sucked into a whole,
Electricity shutting off,
Oreos.
Sickly licorice,
Rich dark chocolate,
Madam's fur coat,
Ink from my fountain pen,
Suffocating chimney smoke,
Black draws out your inner darkness.

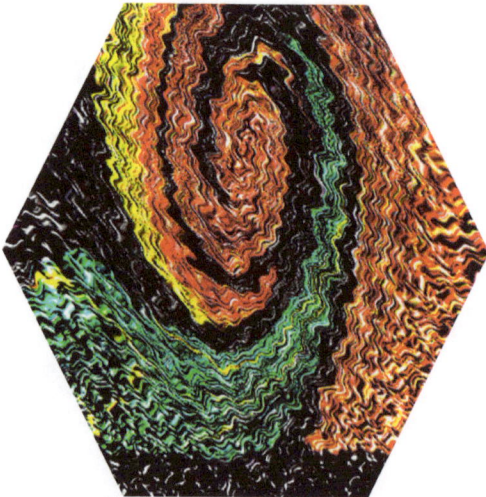

<u>White</u>

Puffy clouds in the sky, Soft cotton balls,
Skin of the fairest of them all,
Snow crunching underneath my boots,
Milk squirting from an udder,
The voices of angels,
Ooey, gooey marshmallows.
Ice cream of sweet vanilla,
Fluffy whipped cream, Sheets
fresh from the dryer, Feathers of
a graceful swan, A glorious wedding
gown, White is purity in the flesh.

<u>Monochrome</u>

Black and white unite
The light and dark join forces
Good against evil Pure against
wicked Gray
The space in between
The best of both worlds It is obsolete.